W9-ACO-201

DISCARD

Date: 3/7/16

J 796.6 RIN
Ringstad, Arnold,
Biking /

PALM BEACH COUNTY
LIBRARY SYSTEM
3650 SUMMIT BLVD.
WEST PALM BEACH, FL 33406

Biking

BY ARNOLD RINGSTAD

Published by The Child's World®
1980 Lookout Drive • Mankato, MN 56003-1705
800-599-READ • www.childsworld.com

Acknowledgments
The Child's World®: Mary Berendes, Publishing Director
Red Line Editorial: Editorial direction
The Design Lab: Design
Amnet: Production

Photographs ©: Mat Hayward/ Shutterstock Images, cover,
20–21; LongQuattro/Shutterstock Images, cover (top right), 10
Cathleen A. Clapper/Shutterstock Images, cover (bottom right),
18; Arvind Balaraman/Thinkstock, back cover (left), 16; Abel
Tumik/Shutterstock Images, back cover (top right), 17; Kitch
Bain/Shutterstock Images, back cover (bottom), 3, 12; BrandX
Pictures, 4–5; Shutterstock Images, 6, 15; Thinkstock, 7; Jacek
Chabraszewski/Shutterstock Images, 9; Rena Schild/Shutterstock
Images, 11; Ugorenkov Aleksandr/Shutterstock Images, 19

Copyright © 2015 by The Child's World®
All rights reserved. No part of this book may be reproduced or
utilized in any form or by any means without written permission
from the publisher.

ISBN 9781626873261
LCCN 2014930660

Printed in the United States of America
Mankato, MN
July, 2014
PA02222

ABOUT THE AUTHOR

Arnold Ringstad lives in Minnesota. He likes to ride his road bike around the bike paths in his city.

CONTENTS

FUN ON TWO WHEELS

Have you ever been **biking**? You might have biked on a dirt path. You may have used a bike to zoom across smooth **pavement**.

Riding a bike is a fun and safe activity.

Maybe you've biked to school. Perhaps you have biked to a friend's house.

People ride bikes in many places. They bike for many reasons. Some people race. Others use bikes for exercise. And some people bike just to have fun. Biking is a fun and exciting way to get around.

WHAT IS BIKING?

Biking is the activity of riding a bicycle. Bikes are called bicycles because they have two wheels. The first bicycles were made in the early 1800s. They were called dandy horses. Early bikes had no pedals. Later in the 1800s, inventors made the first bikes with pedals.

BONESHAKERS

Some early bicycles were nicknamed "boneshakers." They shook riders around when they moved. Boneshakers had hard, iron tires. They did not have the rubber tires we use today. Rubber tires help absorb bumps in the road.

Early bicycles looked unusual. One kind had a huge front wheel. It had a tiny back wheel. Modern-looking bikes came out in the 1880s. They were called safety bicycles. They were safer than earlier bikes. Today, they are just called bicycles.

Early bikes were very different than today's modern ones.

Today's bicycles are safer and more comfortable than older bikes.

PLACES TO RIDE

There are many places to bike. People in cities often bike on roads. Sometimes they ride in the same **lanes** as cars. Other times there are lanes just for bikes.

Many people enjoy riding on bicycle paths. These are smoothly paved areas away from roads. People can bike, run, or walk on these paths.

BIKING TO WORK

Many people drive cars to work. Some choose to ride bikes instead. In the United States, not many people choose to bike. Less than 1 percent of people bike to work. Bikes are more popular in Denmark. In Copenhagen, Denmark's capital, 37 percent of people bike to work.

Others like to bike on dirt paths. These areas are often out in the country. They have rough surfaces. Still, they are lots of fun. Many have big hills. Some even have jumps!

MOUNTAIN OR ROAD?

Different kinds of bicycles are good for different places. Mountain bikes are great for riding on dirt paths. They have wide tires to grip the ground. The tires have knobby surfaces. They give riders control on sand or gravel.

Road bikes are designed for paved roads. Their tires are skinny and smooth. The smooth tires help riders build up speed. Road bikes have special handlebars called drop handlebars. These help bikers ride low and fast.

Road bikes are popular for racing. Racers bike very fast. They go more than 25 miles per hour (40 kmh). One race in France is very long.

It goes more than 2,000 miles (3,219 km)!
The race takes three weeks.

Hybrid bikes are somewhere in the middle.
They have medium-sized tires. The tires help
hybrid bikes work well on and off the road.
Many beginners use hybrid bicycles.

Road bikes are great for racing.

PARTS OF A BIKE

A bicycle has many parts. The frame holds the bike together. The seat, wheels, and handlebars all attach to it. The seat is sometimes called a **saddle**. The rider uses pedals to move the bike forward. A chain connects the pedals to the back wheel.

Many bikes have **gears**. Gears make it easier to climb hills. Riders can switch to a low gear when going uphill. Pedaling becomes easier. They can switch to a higher gear on

A bike's gear controls are on its handlebars.

flat ground. Pedaling is harder, but their speed goes up. Gear controls are usually on the handlebars.

Some bikes have bike computers. The computers attach to the handlebars. The computers also connect to the wheels. Bike computers show riders how far they have ridden. They can also show how fast riders are going. The newest bike computers can connect to apps on smartphones. The apps can map a rider's trip.

HOW BIKE COMPUTERS WORK

Bike computers connect to the wheels. A **sensor** notices when the wheel spins around. Then, it tells the computer. If a 20-inch (51 cm) wheel spins once, the bike has gone 20 inches (51 cm). The computer can figure out distance and speed.

SLOWING DOWN

Moving fast is one thing that makes biking fun. But it is just as important to slow down. That is why bikes have **brakes**. Many bikes have brake controls on their handlebars. The rider squeezes the control. The control pulls a cable. Then, the cable tightens the brake. It grips the wheel. The bike slows down.

There is one brake control on each handlebar. One slows the front wheel. The other slows the back wheel.

Some bikes use a different kind of brake. They are called "kick brakes." Bikes with kick brakes move normally when the rider pedals forward. Pedaling backward activates the brake. This slows the bike down.

Brakes help riders control their speed on hills.

BIKING SAFETY

Biking is lots of fun. But it can be dangerous, too. People who ride bicycles must be careful. Bikers in cities must watch out for cars. Riders in the country must watch out for trees and other **obstacles**. It's important to ride safely and wear safety gear.

One important rule for bikers is to pay attention to the road. They must watch out for anything that might get in their way. Then the biker can slow down or ride

Wear safety gear when you go biking.

around it. Bikers should learn special hand signals. The signals tell cars and other bikers if riders are planning to turn.

It is important to bring water on long bike rides. On hot days, bikers can lose water by sweating. They should drink plenty of water to replace their sweat. Many bikes have a water bottle holder. It keeps a bottle attached to the frame.

Make sure your water bottle will fit in your bottle holder.

SAFETY GEAR

The most important piece of safety gear for bikers is a **helmet**. A helmet is usually made of hard plastic and foam. It protects a rider's head during a crash. Helmets often have vents in them. They help keep riders' heads cool.

Many pieces of safety gear help riders see what's around them. Others tell people

Helmets come in many different styles.

where riders are. Reflectors help car drivers see bikers at night. Bicycle bells let people know riders are nearby. Mirrors let bikers see behind them. All of this gear helps bikers avoid crashing.

SPECIAL HELMETS

Bicycle racers sometimes use helmets with special shapes. They have long, pointed ends. Wind flows smoothly over the pointed ends. This helps the riders move even faster.

Bicycle bells attach to bike handlebars.

BIKING FUN

Biking is a great way to get fresh air and exercise. Bikers get to experience the outdoors all year round. In the spring, riders can bike on mountain trails as flowers bloom. In the summer, they can zoom around on road bikes. In the fall, bikers can ride over crunching

Ride a bike for some outdoor fun!

autumn leaves. And in the winter, riders can pedal mountain bikes through snow and rain.

Having fun and staying safe are what biking is all about. When you have the right gear, you can have a fun, safe ride anywhere. Will you ride through a busy city? Down a bumpy mountain trail? Or maybe on a paved path along the beach? It's up to you!

GLOSSARY

biking (BYEK-ing): Biking is riding on a bicycle. Biking is a fun and safe outdoor activity.

brakes (brAYks): Brakes are parts used to slow a bike down. Brake controls are on the handlebars of many bikes.

gears (gEErz): Gears are parts used to make it easier or harder to pedal. Low gears make it easier to go uphill.

helmet (HEL-mut): A helmet is something worn to protect a rider's head in a crash. A helmet is the most important piece of safety gear for bikers.

hybrid (HYE-bred): If something is hybrid, it is made of a mixture of parts. Hybrid bikes have features of mountain bikes and road bikes.

lanes (lAYnz): Lanes are the parts of roads where one line of cars or bikes travels. Some roads have bikes-only lanes.

obstacles (AHB-stuh-kuls): Obstacles are things that are in the way. Cars and trees are obstacles for bikes.

pavement (PAYV-munt): Pavement is a road or path made of stone or concrete. Road bikes are good for riding on pavement.

saddle (SAD-ul): A saddle is a bicycle seat. A bike saddle is usually made of leather or plastic.

sensor (SEN-sur): A sensor is a device that responds to motion. A sensor notices when a bike's wheel spins around.

TO LEARN MORE

BOOKS

Cole, Steve. *Kids' Easy Bike Care: Tune-Ups, Tools, & Quick Fixes*. Charlotte, VA: Williamson, 2003.

Haduch, Bill. *Go Fly a Bike! The Ultimate Book of Bicycle Fun, Freedom, and Science*. New York: Dutton, 2004.

Herrington, Lisa M. *Bicycle Safety*. New York: Children's Press, 2012.

Mulder, Michelle. *Pedal It! How Bicycles Are Changing the World*. Custer, WA: Orca, 2013.

Raatma, Lucia. *Bicycle Safety*. Mankato, MN: Child's World, 2003.

WEB SITES

Visit our Web site for links about biking:
childsworld.com/links

Note to Parents, Teachers, and Librarians: We routinely verify our Web links to make sure they are safe and active sites. So encourage your readers to check them out!

INDEX